WHERE DO BUTTERFLY COLORS COME FROM?

BUTTERFLY ANATOMY SCIENCE FOR KIDS (LEPIDOPTEROLOGY)

CHILDREN'S BIOLOGICAL SCIENCE OF BUTTERFLIES BOOKS

PRODIGYWIZARD
BOOKS

Butterflies always attract attention. One could not keep himself from not taking a glimpse of these marvellous insects.

Kids love to witness how they glide and sway in the air. But aren't you curious of where they got their striking colors?

Why are they
so colorful?
Find out and
be amazed of
the shimmering
facts about
butterfly colors.

Butterflies display the most brilliant colors of nature. They love to fly and to gather nectar from flower to flower.

As they do
this, one could
witness how
their wings
shimmer and
dance before
your very eyes.
The colors
seem to change
as they flap
their wings.

They change colors for a purpose, like attracting mates, as camouflage and it may signal warning.

It is believed that a butterfly's brilliant colors are taken from two sources. These are taken from the ordinary color and structural color.

The ordinary color comes from normal chemicals that take wavelengths of light and it reflects others. For example the chlorophyll in plants creates green.

Brown
and yellow
butterflies get
their colors
from melanin.
This is what
gives you a tan
color during
summer.

It's more interesting to learn about the structural color of these vibrant insects. It is dependent on the structure of the butterfly's wings.

It is caused by iridescence. As kids, you love to play with bubbles. This happens when light passes through the layers of the bubbles and is reflected several times.

The reflections
add intensity
to the colors.
When you watch
a butterfly it
changes its color
as you move.

A butterfly's wings are composed of scales with multiple layers.

So, when the light passes through or hits the different layers on the scales just imagine how they are reflected several times.

These
reflections and
colors show you
how amazing
these beautiful
insects are.

Can these two sources be combined? Yes, definitely. Combined sources, the structural and the ordinary sources, create intense and brilliant colors.

The combination of colors through reflection is really incredible. Butterflies are really eye-catching.

Everyone will be delighted by their colors. They may seem like simple insects but their vivid and vibrant colors come from complicated and multiple reflections.

Did you enjoy
reading about
butterflies?
Share this to
your friends.